IMAGES
of Ireland

CENTRAL
DUBLIN

The *Irish Times*, which is the oldest of the Dublin newspapers, was first published in 1859. This postcard shows the front page for 3 February 1906 with a view of Sackville Street (O'Connell Street) in the centre. The card was posted in Dublin on 7 August 1907.

The *Irish Independent* was first published on 2 January 1905. It was formed by a merger between the *Irish Daily Independent* and the *Daily Nation*. It also later incorporated the *Freeman's Journal* in 1924. This postcard (*c.* 1907) also shows the front page for Monday 3 February 1906, with a view of the Four Courts in the centre.

IMAGES
of Ireland

CENTRAL
DUBLIN

Compiled by
Derek Stanley

GILL & MACMILLAN

Published in Ireland by
Gill & Macmillan Ltd
Goldenbridge, Dublin 8
with associated companies throughout the world
Copyright © Derek Stanley, 1999

ISBN 0 7171 2956 X

Typesetting and origination by
Tempus Publishing Ltd
Printed in Great Britain by
Midway Clark Printing, Wiltshire

The coat of arms was granted to the City of Dublin in 1607 following a visit by Daniel Molyneux, Ulster King of Arms and Principal Herald of All Ireland. This card, postmarked 17 February 1906, shows three castles on a shield – to the right there is a female figure representing 'law', holding an erect sword in her right hand and an olive branch in her left hand, and to the left there is a female figure representing 'justice', holding a pair of scales in her left hand and an olive branch in her right hand. The City's motto is *Obedientia civium urbis felicitas*, which roughly translates 'The City's happiness depends on the people's loyalty'.

Contents

Acknowledgements   6

Introduction   7

1.   The River Liffey and its Banks   9

2.   The City Centre   31

3.   Events   59

4.   Sport, People, Health and Recreation   81

5.   Around the Suburbs   105

Acknowledgements

I am grateful to Pat O'Brien for his help, advice and encouragement. I should also like to thank Des Quail for allowing me to use some postcards from his own collection.

I would like to acknowledge and thank my friends and family who helped me by lending photographs, sharing memories and searching out information, especially Dr George Corbett, Joseph Corbett, Marie Corbett, Pauline Dempsey, Seamus Kearns, Fergal MacAlister, Joan O'Byrne, Peter O'Hara.

I owe a special debt of appreciation to my wife Theresa, who provided me with unstinting support.

Dublin Traffic – a comic postcard which was posted in Dublin on 19 May 1907. At that time, trams and horse-drawn vehicles were still the main form of transport. However, the motor car was becoming more popular. The speed limit for cars was 20mph. Today in Dublin there are no trams, but traffic congestion is such that most car journeys would still be within this limit!

Introduction

Dublin is a 'special' city, with roots in over a thousand years of history. Some of the more recent historical events are recalled in this book. The images recall events of importance, the buildings and those who lived and worked in this great European city.

The constant driving force in Dublin is the people, who warmly welcome every visitor, talk freely, laugh often and at times complain about their lot. However, all Dubliners love freedom, and that right, which includes free speech, is to them a necessity of life. It is not surprising that the city has produced so many great authors and playwrights as everybody has an 'opinion' and all have tales to tell.

It is hoped that this range of photographs and old postcards from the author's collection will bring enjoyment to all. The text is not exhaustive and together with the images should be used only as a guide. Perusing each section may well arouse interest and inspire a search for more information about aspects of the city's history. Of necessity, in a book of this size, not all areas can be covered in detail. The aim is to give a 'flavour' of the city and to portray that in each section.

The photographs have been chosen to represent areas, events, people and the social history of the city. Looking at the photographs should evoke memories of past events for those who have experienced them at first hand. For those too young to remember, and for newcomers to Dublin, the images will give some insight into the history and events which have contributed to the culture of this unique city. We are fortunate that the work of local photographers in the early part of the century and postcards produced at that time are still available today. These images have become a valuable record and source of information, helping to preserve the past for future generations.

The book is a pictorial account of Dublin within recent memory which may bring some sadness when we remember people and places that have gone. However, as with any family album, there will be photographs in the collection which will bring pleasure and enjoyment as happier times or events which changed the course of history are recalled. Memories are precious and it would be praise indeed if this book were given a place on the bookshelf with the family photograph album.

Derek Stanley, 1999

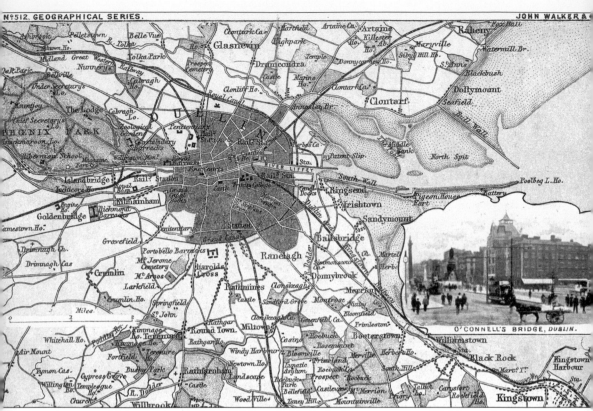

A postcard from a series by John Walker & Co. Ltd, showing a map of Dublin and its environs, *c.* 1903. The city is compact and enjoys many natural advantages as it is sheltered by mountains to the south, while to the east there is Dublin Bay and the Irish Sea. The River Liffey runs through the middle, with the Royal Canal forming a semi-circular ring on the north side and the Grand Canal completing the curve on the south side.

One

The River Liffey
and its Banks

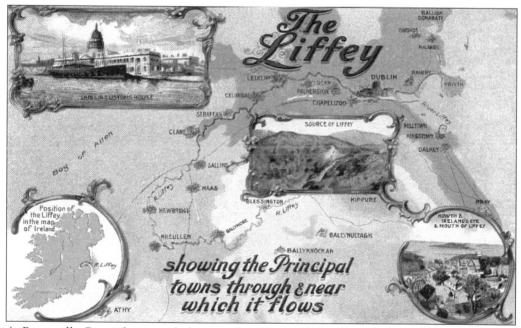

A Bournville Reward postcard showing the course of the River Liffey, which rises in the Wicklow mountains at Kippure, thirteen miles from Dublin and only nine miles from the sea. However, it flows in a great loop through Wicklow and Kildare, giving it a total length of seventy miles before it reaches the sea at Dublin Bay. The river is tidal up to the weir at Islandbridge. It bisects the City of Dublin from west to east into almost equal parts. This section will show some of the places of interest on both banks of the river.

The Royal Hospital, Kilmainham, sited on the south bank of the Liffey, *c.* 1905. It was designed by Sir William Robinson and, like Wren's Chelsea Hospital, was based on Louis XIV's home for old soldiers, 'Les Invalides' in Paris. It was built in 1684 costing the then very large sum of £24,000 and has fine high rooms with long corridors and a spacious arcaded courtyard.

Royal Hospital and Inmates, Kilmainham

The old soldiers, *c.* 1901: some of the 300 old and disabled veterans in their distinctive uniforms, who were resident at the Royal Hospital. The hospital remained an old soldiers' home until 1927. It was then used as the Garda headquarters until 1950. It lay empty for some time, but was restored in the 1980s by the Office of Public Works. Since 1991, it has been the home of the Irish Museum of Modern Art.

10

Kingsbridge Station, Dublin

Great Southern station, Kingsbridge (Heuston station), *c.* 1906. This very fine Victorian railway station was built in 1845 using local granite to the design of Sancton Wood. It has the look of a great Renaissance house with its Corinthian pillars. Due to a stonemasons' strike, the building was completed four years late. The station was renamed Heuston station in 1966 in honour of Sean Heuston, an employee of the company, who was executed after the Easter Rising in 1916. It was used as the location for scenes in the film *The Great Train Robbery*.

A long goods train '101' class 0-6-0 No. 144, with horse boxes and wagons, leaving Kingsbridge under steam for the south of Ireland, *c.* 1915. The station yard foreman, the train driver and his assistant pose for the photographer.

Dr Steevens's Hospital was founded in 1720 by Grizel Steevens with the estate bequeathed by her brother Richard, who was Professor of Medicine at Trinity College. The architect was Thomas Burgh, who designed the library at Trinity. The hospital, which was the oldest in Ireland, opened in 1733 and closed in the 1990s. The site had been chosen away from the city centre to try to isolate the hospital from areas of fever and infection.

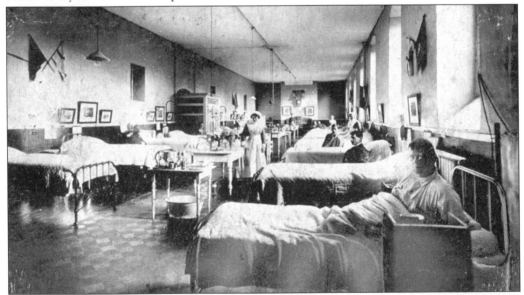

Madam Steevens's ward, c. 1905, showing the typical long hospital ward for male patients. The ward was named after Grizel Steevens, the founder, who lived in the hospital until her death in 1747, aged ninety-two. She carried out charitable work always wearing a heavy veil, so as not to be recognized. However, Dubliners at the time said that she had been born with a pig's face because her mother, while pregnant, had refused to help a beggar woman. A curse had then been laid on Grizel, the unborn child.

An aerial view of Guinness's Brewery, which was founded in 1759 by Arthur Guinness who moved his business from Leixlip, Co. Kildare. It occupies a site of around sixty acres on three levels and is one of Europe's largest breweries. This postcard shows the malt stores, breweries and vat houses in the foreground and behind these, are the racking sheds and cooperage yard. In the background are the quays on the River Liffey.

Guinness's Brewery, c. 1910, showing the decorated dray-horses looking smart with polished brasses in the yard waiting for their carts to be loaded. In 1908, the firm had 171 horses, 210 drays and floats, all in full use. In the background, across the river, can be seen the Royal Barracks.

Empty casks were unloaded at Scald Bank and many were transported on the miniature narrow-gauge (22-inch) railway system, which ran through the brewery site on over seven miles of railway track. There was also a broad-gauge system, with a connecting line of the Great Southern and Western Railway, which ran from the cooperage area to Kingsbridge station.

The cask filling department in the brewery. The casks were made in the cooperage and in 1908 were produced almost entirely by hand at the rate of 1,500 a week. The life of each cask was about ten years.

The racking room in the brewery where the casks were racked and filled with stout. In 1908 the amount brewed was the equivalent of two gallons per head of population in Britain and Ireland. The total number of staff and employees at the Brewery in 1907 was about 3,240.

Loading the drays and floats on the lower level, c. 1918. The barrels were loaded according to their destination on dray, boat or railway.

The fleet of Guinness motor lorries and their drivers gather in the yard of the brewery, *c.* 1925. The lorries were a familiar sight on the roads, although drays continued to be used for deliveries in the city.

Guiness's Wharf, Dublin

Shewing how the famous Dublin Stout is dispatched down the Liffey

Guinness's wharf at Victoria Quay, *c.* 1908, showing the steam barges being loaded with casks to be taken down the Liffey to the Channel steamers anchored at the North Wall. In 1908, the company had ten steamers working on the river. Their funnels had to be lowered when passing under the bridges at high tide. Kingsbridge station is seen in the distance.

The Iveagh Markets on Francis Street, *c.* 1917. They were designed by Frederick Hicks, built with an impressive façade of limestone and brick, and opened in 1907. The archways each have a fine carved keystone head representing the various nations around the world. However, one bearded head over an archway on the southern façade has an impish grin and is said to represent Lord Iveagh, the Guinness chairman and benefactor.

Dolphin's Barn on the South Circular Road near Camac Bridge on the Grand Canal, *c.* 1920. This is part of the Liberties and is joined by Cork Street to the oldest part of the city. Our Lady of Dolours church, built of granite, was opened in 1893 and has an unusual four-sided tower.

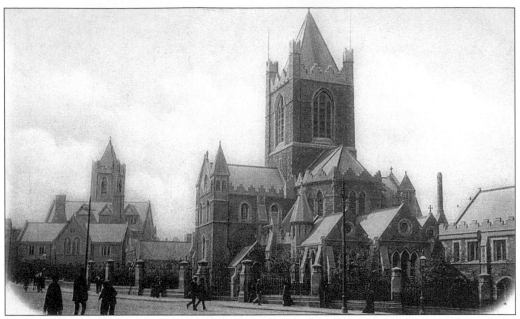

Christchurch Cathedral, *c.* 1905. Overlooking the Liffey, the cathedral is on the site of a wooden church built in 1038 by Sitric Silkenbeard, the Norse King of Dublin. In the 1170s, Strongbow, Earl of Pembroke, and Archbishop St Laurence O'Toole rebuilt the cathedral using stone and a further restoration was carried out in the 1870s. Today the vaulted crypt contains the stocks of the Liberty of Christchurch. The stocks date from 1670, when the Dean was in charge of the district and they were used to punish people committing crimes.

St Patrick's Cathedral, *c.* 1914. The cathedral is built on the oldest Christian site in Dublin and St Patrick is said to have baptized some converts there around AD 450. John Comyn, Archbishop of Dublin, began building the church in 1191 and it became a cathedral in 1213. However, much of the original construction was destroyed in a fire in the fourteenth century and had to be rebuilt. Jonathan Swift, author of *Gulliver's Travels* and a champion of the poor, who was Dean from 1713 to 1745, is buried in the cathedral.

Weaver's Square, seen here around 1905, is in the area of the Liberties, the centre of the silk, poplin and wool hand-loom weaving trade, which dated back to the 1690s, when many Huguenots settled in Dublin. The poplin was of very high quality. Dublin poplin-makers refused to allow anyone who had not served a seven-year apprenticeship, or who was not the eldest son of a poplin-maker, to work as a poplin-weaver. J. Gaffney's shop is at the far end of the cobbled square. The message on the card says that the buildings are about to be cleared away.

Dilapidated, overcrowded buildings due for demolition in Poole Street in the area of the Coombe, c. 1905. In the Liberties during the nineteenth century there was much poverty, with no plumbing, sanitation or regular water supply. Tenement houses often sheltered many families, each occupying one room. There were frequent salmonella and typhus epidemics and the mortality rate was high.

The old Music Hall in Fishamble Street, Dublin, where the "Messiah" was first performed.

THE MUSIC HALL, Fishamble Street, was founded in 1741, by the Bull's Head Musical Society, and in the same and following year, HANDEL performed there, under the patronage of the Lord Lieutenant and the Court. It continued the most fashionable place of public entertainment until the close of last century. After many vicissitudes, it was in 1868 added to KENNAN & SONS' Works, and it now resounds again with the "Harmonious Blacksmith," differently composed.

Advertisement for Kennan & Sons at 13-25 Fishamble Street, c. 1910. The view also shows the Music Hall where the *Messiah* was first performed by Handel on 13 April 1742. In fact, for the performance, the hall was too small for the expected crowd and ladies were asked not to wear hooped skirts and gentlemen not to wear their swords. The street derives its name from the fish stalls or shambles, which traded there in the tenth century, when it was the pathway from the Viking port of Dublin to High Street, the principal trading street.

An advertisement from around 1910 for an elocutionist, a Mr W.D. Brockhill, 'willing to perform at Socials, Parties & Concerts', who lived at Chaworth Place, off the South Circular Road. He would have had a wealth of literature to choose from as nineteenth-century Dublin produced and inspired so many great writers and poets.

Chapelizod, c. 1905. This was a popular village on the north bank of the Liffey, whose name is said to derive from Isolde, lover of Tristan in the medieval romance, whose brother, the King of Ireland, was killed by Tristan. The Dublin Whiskey Distillery is on the far left. This was powered by a large waterwheel on the Liffey. It is of interest that John Joyce, father of James Joyce, lived in the white house next to the distillery when he was secretary of the company in 1877.

A smartly dressed party setting out from Chapelizod in November 1908. They are riding on an outside car pulled by a single horse. The passengers were open to the weather and their legs dangled down outside the pair of wheels to a foot-board.

The main entrance to Phoenix Park, which covers 1,752 acres and is the largest walled park in any European city. It dates from the 1670s and has a herd of 450 deer. The Wellington Monument, which is 67m high and the largest obelisk in Europe, is on the far left. It was erected in 1861 to commemorate the victories of Dubliner Arthur Wellesley, Duke of Wellington, particularly over Napoleon Bonaparte at Waterloo.

Boys on parade at the Royal Hibernian Military School, Phoenix Park, *c.* 1905. This was founded in 1764 and was originally a boarding school for the maintenance and education of soldiers' children. Many of the boys would themselves fight in the First World War. The building is now occupied by St Mary's Hospital for the elderly.

The Band and Pipers of the Cameron Highlanders at the Royal Barracks, *c.* 1907. The barracks were designed by Thomas Burgh and built in 1704. They were then the largest in the world and could accommodate 5,000 men, to include four foot battalions and one of horse. Until it was decommissioned in 1996, this was the world's oldest purpose-built barracks in continuous occupation. The National Museum of Ireland now displays part of its collection in the building.

A Corpus Christi Procession around 1950 at the Lourdes Grotto, St Mary of the Angels, Church Street. Soldiers provide the guard of honour. The present church of the Franciscan Capuchin Fathers was completed in 1881 and the private chapel of the Third Order of St Francis was built in 1891.

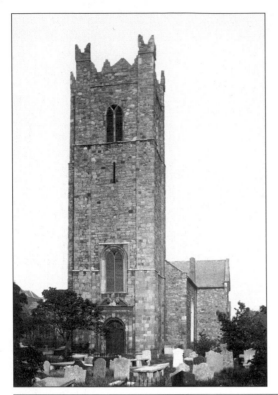

St Michan's church in Church Street, c. 1910. This church was originally built by the Vikings in 1096 and was extensively rebuilt in 1686. It has a superb organ upon which Handel played in 1742. One of the church vaults, which have limestone walls and dry air, contains four naturally mummified bodies in their coffins from the seventeenth century. One of the bodies is that of a crusader whose legs had to be broken after death so that he would fit in his coffin. Another vault holds the coffins of the Sheares brothers, executed for their part in the 1798 Rising.

The Four Courts, c. 1929. Situated on the north bank of the Liffey, the Courts were designed by Thomas Cooley, who died before work started in 1785. After his death, James Gandon took over and modified the design. The building was not completed until 1802. It actually has five courts radiating out from a central domed rotunda. After being damaged during the Civil War (see p. 74), the Four Courts were rebuilt in 1931.

The King's Inns, Dublin.

The King's Inns, Henrietta Street, was designed by James Gandon and not completed until 1827, after his death. The dining room is original. It has not been altered, nor was it damaged in the Rebellion or Civil War, which was the fate of so many interiors in Dublin buildings designed by Gandon. During their training, barristers used to live in and study at the Inns. This custom has changed, but now it is necessary for them to attend a number of dinners at the King's Inns during their pupillage, before qualification as barristers.

VIEW ALONG THE QUAYS FROM O'CONNELL BRIDGE, DUBLIN

A view up the Liffey from O'Connell Bridge in around 1950, showing the Wellington cast-iron footbridge, which was built in 1816 and commonly known as the 'Halfpenny Bridge' due to the toll which was charged for using the bridge. The charge ceased in 1919. It was renamed the Liffey Bridge in 1922. The view shows cars and buses on the quays, although horse-drawn vehicles are still in evidence.

The Ballast Office, *c.* 1910. This was sited on Aston Quay, overlooking O'Connell Bridge. Its clock was regarded by Dubliners as the most reliable timepiece in the city. From 1801, the office was occupied by the Ballast Board, which imposed and collected charges and had the responsibility for preserving and improving the port. In 1867, the Ballast Board was replaced by the Dublin Port and Docks Board. The Board stayed at this office until 1981.

A busy scene on the Quays, *c.* 1928. In the centre, the number 24 tram with a fairly full top deck passes the Wireless Stores on Bachelor's Walk. A Garda controls the traffic on O'Connell Bridge. In the distance, on the Liffey, can be seen the Butt Swing Bridge and behind that the Loopline Railway Bridge, disliked by Dubliners, as it spoils the view of the Custom House from O'Connell Bridge.

The old Butt Swing Bridge and the Loopline Railway Bridge, c. 1900. The Swivel or Swing Bridge was constructed in 1879 and would open to allow ships through to Burgh Quay and Eden Quay. However, in 1890 the Loopline Railway Bridge was built downstream. This railway bridge prevented access for large ships, which then had to berth at the Custom House Quay. The Swivel Bridge had too narrow a carriageway, and the present Butt Bridge was built to replace it in 1932.

Cross-channel steamers loading at the Custom House Quay, c. 1920. The loaded Guinness barges are seen on the river. On the quay is the magnificent Custom House Building, which was designed by James Gandon and finished in 1791. It took ten years to build as there were difficulties building on reclaimed swamp land and also public opposition to the move downstream from the old Custom House at Essex Quay.

Dublin Docks in around 1920, showing much activity with ships berthed in the foreground at the Liverpool Steamers sheds. Further down the South Wall, there are more ships at the British and Irish Steam Packet Company sheds. On the opposite side of the Liffey, boats are berthed at the North Wall.

BRITISH AND IRISH STEAM PACKET COMPANY, LIMITED, DUBLIN.

S.S. LADY Roberts 5/Sept 1905

The SS *Lady Roberts*, *c.* 1905. This steamer carried steerage and first-class passengers for the British and Irish Steam Packet Company from London to Dublin, calling at Portsmouth, Southampton, Plymouth and Falmouth. It was a long sea trip, but the company continued to operate a service on this route until 1933.

The SS *Hibernia*, c. 1905. This was one of four express steamers based at Holyhead, which carried passengers and freight each night to Dublin (North Wall) and each day to Dun Laoghaire on behalf of the London and North Western Railway company. During the First World War, the *Hibernia* was requisitioned, and renamed HMS *Tara*. It was sunk in the Mediterranean in 1915 by a German U-boat.

The Captain, officers and crew of the SS *Hibernia*, c. 1904. The solitary female member of the crew provided nursing services and must sometimes have felt very isolated.

Dublin Docks in around 1950, showing a group of dockers working in a ship's hold filling the giant crane buckets (tubs) with coal, using No. 5 shovels. From left to right: Johnny Montgomery, Blake Montgomery, Val Butler, Johnny Farrell, Willie Rodgers, Peter McDonald, Christy Robinson, Barry Lennon, Joe Smith, Jim McDonald, and Sam Dunne.

The mouth of the Liffey around 1905, showing a paddle steamer with two funnels heading up the river. Masted sailing ships are berthed further out. The cranes used for loading and unloading ships stand on the South Wall of the quays. The rowing-boat may be a ferry service operating in the lower river.

Two
The City Centre

O'Connell Bridge and Street, *c.* 1910. The O'Connell Monument is in the centre with Nelson's Pillar in the distance. The bridge is as wide as it is long and has double tramlines. On the right, the building with the unusual tower and spire is the Dublin Bread Company Restaurant, designed by George Beckett and opened in 1901. The building had to be demolished after being damaged in the 1916 Rising.

The O'Connell Monument, seen here around 1905, was designed by John Foley who died in 1874. The sculpture was then finished by his assistant, Thomas Brock, and unveiled in 1882. Standing by the statue is one of the Dublin Metropolitan Police, who were known as the 'giant police' as they were all over six feet tall, carried batons and wore large spiked helmets. They were amalgamated with the Garda Síochána in 1925. The force stopped wearing helmets in 1950.

O'Connell St. Dublin (from Nelson Pillar).

Photo Lafayette

A view of Lower O'Connell Street from Nelson's Pillar, c. 1926. Trams of the Dublin United Tram Company, in the centre, head away from the Pillar. Horse-drawn and motor traffic is in the outer lanes. Dublin streets were tarred for the first time in 1909, following complaints that motor cars were throwing up too much dirt and dust at other road users and pedestrians.

The Metropole Hotel, *c.* 1915. This was a popular Dublin hotel from the middle of the nineteenth century onwards. The Mitchell family purchased the hotel from the Jury family in 1892 and added the ironwork balconies. Situated next to the GPO, the hotel was destroyed in the fighting in 1916. It was not until 5 February 1922 that a new Metropole ballroom and cinema complex was opened on the site.

Clery's store, O'Connell Street, *c.* 1940. This popular department store, designed by Ashlin and Coleman, was opened on 9 August 1922. It was built on the site of the Imperial Hotel and the original Clery's Dublin Drapery Warehouse (founded in 1883), which had been destroyed in the 1916 Rising.

The General Post Office, *c.* 1915. The building was designed by Francis Johnston and opened in 1818. It cost the very large sum at that time of £50,000 to build. Thomas Kirk from Cork was the sculptor for the statues over the entrance, which portray Fidelity, Hibernia and Mercury. Before this he had been the sculptor for Nelson's statue on the top of the Pillar. The Pillar had been built before the GPO in 1808 at a cost of £6,857.

Flower sellers at Nelson's Pillar, *c.* 1905. Outdoor traders have been a feature of the city's life since medieval times. This was the ideal site, as the trams stopped here and it was near to Henry Street and the large stores in O'Connell Street.

Trams gathered at Nelson's Pillar, c. 1945. The Dublin United Tramways Company was formed in 1881. The trams were a popular form of transport and the company had over 300 trams by 1915, most running to and from Nelson's Pillar. However, as elsewhere, their popularity declined and all the trams were withdrawn in Dublin in 1949.

Henry Street, looking towards Nelson's Pillar, c. 1920. This was named after Henry Moore, first Earl of Drogheda, and is one of Dublin's main shopping streets. On the right, a truck is parked outside Cochrane's. Further up the street on that side can be seen the entrance canopy for Arnott's store, occupying Nos 9-15 Henry Street.

Henry Street, *c.* 1910. A four-wheeled brougham is parked outside No. 36, which has a ladies' hairdressing salon on the ground floor with the dentist, M. McDonnell, on the first floor. People are shopping next door at No. 37, E. Marks & Co., the original 'penny bazaar'.

The Gresham Hotel, *c.* 1945. The original hotel dating from 1817 was destroyed in the Civil War and rebuilt in 1927. It is well known for its fine ballroom. A little further down towards the Pillar is the Savoy Cinema, which was built in 1929 as the biggest picture house in Ireland. It could hold up to 3,000 people. Dubliners loved the cinema and at that time Dublin had more cinema seats per head of population than any city in Europe.

The Rotunda or 'Round Room', *c*. 1907. This opened in 1767 and was designed by John Ensor. He was inspired by Jones's Rotunda at Ranelagh Gardens in Chelsea. The entrance block, which joins it to the street, was added later by James Gandon. Profits from events and entertainments at the Rotunda and the Assembly Rooms went to support the Rotunda Hospital. The hospital is to the left. It opened in 1757 and was the first maternity hospital in these isles. It has a world-wide reputation and is still going strong.

The Parnell Monument and the Rotunda, *c*. 1912. The Rotunda has now become a cinema and is showing a film called *The Sea Beast*. The Parnell Monument, erected in 1911, has a dominant position at this end of O'Connell Street. The 'outside' cars queue by the monument, waiting for passengers, while the No. 11 Clonskeagh tram heads towards the Pillar.

Belvedere College, from North St George's Street, *c.* 1915. The mansion was built by Michael Stapleton in 1786 for the second Earl of Belvedere and purchased by the Jesuits in 1841. The rooms contain very fine Adam plasterwork. The college has had many famous pupils including James Joyce, who went there in 1888 at the age of eleven, Kevin Barry and Cathal Brugha.

Great Denmark Street and the Post Office, *c.* 1914. Belvedere College is on the right and the Abbey Presbyterian church, known always as 'Findlater's church' after the wealthy grocer who endowed it, is at the end of the street. This neo-Gothic landmark dates from 1864.

St Francis Xavier church, *c.* 1917. This church, designed by John B. Keane, is on Upper Gardiner Street between terraced houses. It has an Ionic portico and was built in 1829 in the style of the Jesuit church in Rome. The Parish Hall, near the church, was the headquarters of the Pioneer Total Abstinence Association, founded in 1898 by Fr James Cullen SJ, whose members all wear the distinctive lapel badge of the Sacred Heart.

The Pro-Cathedral, Marlborough Street, seen here around 1907, was built between 1815 and 1825. The original site suggested was on O'Connell Street, where the GPO now stands. However, this was before Catholic Emancipation in 1829, and it was thought that such a prominent site for the cathedral could provoke anti-Catholic feeling. It was here that Newman publicly announced his conversion to Catholicism in 1851. The celebrated tenor, Count John McCormack (1884-1945), was once a member of the Cathedral Palestrina Choir.

The Great Northern Railway terminus, Amiens Street, *c.* 1905. This looks Italian, with its imposing central tower. It was designed by William Dean Butler in 1844. The station was renamed Connolly Station in 1966 to commemorate James Connolly, one of the leaders of the 1916 Rising.

The Belfast train under steam leaving Amiens Street station, *c.* 1940. The locomotive is No. 87, the *Kestrel*, one of the three-cylinder compounds built by the Great Northern Railway in 1932.

O'Connell Bridge and D'Olier Street, *c.* 1905. The fine stone-built Carlisle Building, which held the *Irish Independent* offices, stood on the corner of D'Olier Street and Burgh Quay. It was demolished in the 1960s and O'Connell Bridge House was built in its place.

The Dublin Coffee Palace, 6 Townsend Street, *c.* 1907. This was a popular temperance hotel and restaurant, which did not sell alcohol. In the city it was recognized that drunkenness was the source of many family problems, and groups such as the Dublin Total Abstinence Society ran regular temperance meetings.

Westmoreland Street with its Georgian buildings, looking towards O'Connell Bridge, *c.* 1915. Model T Ford cars are parked outside the shops. Both this street and D'Olier Street were laid out, around 1800, by the Wide Streets Commissioners, who by their planning, improved many central Dublin streets. However, some of their planned reforms never took place and there are still streets in Dublin like Capel Street, as narrow as they were 200 years ago.

Looking to Westmoreland Street from College Green, *c.* 1925. On the left, is the portico for the House of Lords, designed by James Gandon and built in 1789. The statue of Edmund Burke, the eighteenth-century political philosopher, is seen on the right looking out over the Green. A schoolboy prepares to mount the No. 15 Terenure tram.

The West Front of Trinity College, c. 1920. The impressive Palladian frontage was designed by Theodore Jacobson in 1750 and is a perfect balance to the Parliament Building on College Green. A horse-drawn cart is seen on the right carrying crates to Jacob's biscuit factory in Bishop Street.

An aerial view of Trinity College taken by Norman Ashe around 1951, showing the squares, buildings and College Park. It is an 'oasis' in the centre of Dublin. The Campanile bell tower in the centre overlooks Parliament Square. On the right, behind the circular 'Reading Room' is the Library with its great Long Room which houses the Brian Boru harp and the Book of Kells. Trinity Library, like Oxford and Cambridge, is a copyright library and receives a free copy of every book published in Britain and Ireland.

Degree Day College Rag, *c.* 1940. Students in fancy dress on the steps of the Graduates Memorial Building with staff looking on. Each year the students would hold a parade to raise money for charity. It was not until 1904 that women students were admitted to Trinity, but by 1914 they already amounted to 16 per cent of the students on the college books. The first woman professor was appointed in 1934.

The procession of students gathers. They appear to have gone to a great deal of trouble with their costumes. However, some of them would not be politically correct today!

The Provost with a group of staff from Trinity in College Park in the summer of 1930.

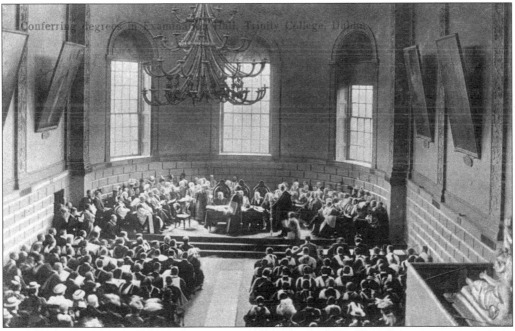

Conferring of Degrees in the Examination Hall, c. 1907. The magnificent sixty-light chandelier, which was once in the Old Parliament House on College Green, hangs from the ceiling. The hall is still used for students who are sitting their examinations.

Graduates on the steps of the Chapel, after receiving their medical degrees, July 1945. The tall central figure is Harry Lee Parker, lecturer and consultant neurologist. Only some of the graduates are identified. In the back row: Bob Graham. Middle row: George Corbett, Llewellyn Jones and Peter Daly. Front row: Betty Carlisle, Barbara Stokes and David Walsh.

A happy group of medical students on the Chapel steps after receiving BA degrees in 1967. From left to right, back row: S. Forbes, G. Hunter, D. Alford , D. Stanley, H. Brewster, D. Bowie, I. Ritchie, G. May, R. O'Connor. Middle row: C. Spratt, S. Bell, M. Smith, A. Nolan, K. Jordan. Front row: M. Doherty, C. De Wolfe De Wytt, H. Rose, H. Ring, L. St John Jones, M. Street, M. Franklin, S. O'Connor, P. Doyle.

College Green, *c.* 1912. The Bank of Ireland was designed by Sir Edward Pearce and completed in 1731. The Irish Parliament met here until the Act of Union in 1801. After this, the country was governed from Westminster and, in 1803, the building was sold to the Bank of Ireland for £40,000. A condition of the sale was that the interior should be changed, so that the rooms could no longer be used for public debate. The only room which is much the same today is the panelled House of Lords room.

College Green, *c.* 1918. The statue of King William of Orange, on its high pedestal, faces down Dame Street. This statue was often vandalized and in 1836 a bomb caused serious damage with the King losing his head, left arm and leg. This was repaired, but in 1929 a further bomb destroyed the statue.

Dame Street, *c.* 1910. The name derives from a dam on the river Poddle beside Dublin Castle. In the eighteenth century, this was the trading centre for the city's goldsmiths and an important centre for commerce, banking and insurance. Just like today, people needed tempting with the promise of 'bargains' and on the right, the jewellers, B. Hyam, advertise their 'great rebuilding sale'.

Dame Street, *c.* 1910, looking down towards City Hall. There are many fine Georgian buildings in this busy commercial street.

The City Hall, Dame Street, with its Corinthian portico, c. 1926. It was designed by Thomas Cooley and originally built in 1769 as the Royal Exchange, in which the Dublin Guild of Merchants transacted business. The Lord Mayor of Dublin moved there in 1852.

An aerial view of Dublin Castle taken by Norman Ashe, c. 1951. The City Hall, with its domed rotunda, is seen on the right. The Castle was built around 1204 on high ground south of the Liffey. It had circular towers at its corners and a surrounding moat filled by the River Poddle. Only part of the Record Tower, in the centre next to the chapel, is left from the original Norman castle.

St Patrick's Day in 1905, as Trooping the Colour takes place in the Upper Castle Yard. The Lord Lieutenant and his entourage gather on the balcony. The tower above them was the first public building in Ireland to have a clock, which was presented by Queen Elizabeth I. This was a special day and on 17 March every year, the 'Castle Season' would end with a banquet at the castle and the St Patrick's Ball.

Nursing and medical staff of Dublin Castle Red Cross Hospital, c. 1916. During the First World War, the Drawing Room and other rooms in the Castle were used as a Red Cross military hospital for wounded troops, including Irishmen fighting for the British Army. In the week of the Easter Rising, the hospital worked at full stretch, treating 118 wounded soldiers, 34 rebels, 20 civilians and two policemen, with 36 deaths.

South Great George's Street, looking back towards Dame Street, *c.* 1920. In the distance, on the right, is the towered frontage of the South City Markets, which had opened as the city's first large shopping centre in 1881. However, after being burned down in August 1892, it was rebuilt with an arcade instead of a hall and re-opened in 1894. The view shows a farmer, probably coming from the cattle market, leading a cow up the road. The Soldiers' Home, which provided recreational facilities for the troops, is on the right.

Aungier Street, *c.* 1919. This street leads from South Great George's Street to Redmond's Hill. Thomas Moore, composer and poet (1779-1852), was born at No. 12 and lived there for twenty years. Here his father kept a grocery shop, while Moore wrote poems in a room on the first floor. He is best known for his melody *The Last Rose of Summer.*

Nassau Street, looking towards the bottom of Grafton Street, *c.* 1905. The street is named after the Count of Nassau. On the right, inside the railed walls of Trinity, which run the whole length of the street, is the superb Provost's House, built by John Smyth in 1759, at a cost of £11,000.

Dawson Street which links Nassau Street and St Stephen's Green, *c.* 1914. Two trams are at the corner on the north side of the Green: the right-hand one is heading for Terenure and the left to the Pillar. The trams were a good method of transport, but the drivers and conductors, together with the upper deck passengers, were very open to the weather.

Looking up Grafton Street, which links College Green and St Stephen's Green, *c.* 1910. The street is busy with shoppers. On the left Yeates and Son, one of the many jewellers in the area, has a prime spot at the junction with Nassau Street.

Brown Thomas & Co., *c.* 1920. This well-known department store, with its fine Victorian frontage, was sited at 15-17 Grafton Street. The store originally opened as a haberdashery in 1849, selling high-class silks and clothing. The shop flourished and expanded so that by 1900 over 300 staff were employed. It became one of Dublin's most fashionable stores.

Grafton Street looking back towards Trinity College, *c.* 1907. It was a very fashionable shopping street. On the left are shops selling silver and jewellery. At No. 86 is Moore & Co. and at No. 87 is Jameson's, with the offices of the *Daily Express* Servants Registry above. At Nos 88-91 is Switzer's, which sold quality clothes to ladies and gentlemen. Switzer, a Swiss immigrant, had opened a small shop in Grafton Street in 1838. He built up a good reputation so the business thrived and it became one of Ireland's largest department stores.

Grafton Street, *c.* 1950. The cars head in a one-way system towards Stephen's Green. Today, the transport scene has changed and the street is crowded with pedestrians.

Grafton Street, *c.* 1905. A superb car with solid tyres, a French De Dion Bouton, watched by shoppers, heads up the street. At that time, before the introduction of the Model T Ford in 1910, cars were very expensive, costing around £1,000. The delivery cart on the left advertises Crane & Sons, well known in Dublin for their fine selection of pianos and organs.

The upper end of Grafton Street, *c.* 1944, showing the Royal Dublin Fusiliers' Memorial Arch entrance to St Stephen's Green. This twenty-two acre park, with its lakes and waterfall, is beautifully laid out and has been a popular attraction for Dubliners since it was re-opened to the public in 1877. In that year, an Act of Parliament was introduced by Sir Arthur Guinness, who also paid for the restoration and landscaping of the park.

Stephen's Green North, *c*. 1910. A two-wheeled trap heads in the direction of the Shelbourne Hotel. On the left is A. Bell & Sons, Dyers and Cleaners. The Dublin Bread Company shop is next door at No. 3, with a horse-drawn van standing outside.

The Shelbourne Hotel, *c*. 1920. This fine Victorian hotel, with its statues of Nubian princesses at the entrance and slave girls at the front corners, opened in 1867. Due to its superb location overlooking the Green, it was the fashionable society hotel for the Dublin Season and had many famous guests including Shelley and also Thackeray, who was extremely impressed during his stay in 1842.

National University, Earlsfort Terrace, c. 1940. The classical-fronted building was originally built in 1863 and behind it was the Winter Gardens, a glass palace for the International Exhibition in May 1865. The Winter Gardens were later demolished and in 1908 the building was redesigned by R.M. Butler, for the National University, with University College Dublin as one of its constituent colleges.

National University Degree Day Rag, 1924. Collecting for charity, hooded students walk through puddles escorting a car, which has a motley assortment of uniformed officers. The crowd has gathered to watch, but some look a little puzzled at the outfits.

The Dáil Chamber, Leinster House, Dublin

The Dáil Chamber, Leinster House, Kildare Street. The mansion was built by Richard Cassels for Lord Kildare in 1745. It was purchased by the Royal Dublin Society in 1815. They sold it to the government for the sum of £68,000 in 1922, and it became the meeting place for the Chamber of Deputies and the Senate.

Westland Row   Dublin

Westland Row, c. 1910. A train is seen on the cast-iron railway bridge heading for Westland Row (now Pearse) railway station. The bridge was one of those built in the 1890s to connect the Northern and Southern railway systems. The impressive St Andrew's church, built by James Bolger in 1832, is on the right. Following the Catholic Emancipation Act in 1829, this was the first Catholic church to be built on a main street. James Joyce called the church All Hallows when it was visited by Mr Bloom in *Ulysses*.

Three

Events

The Irish Peace Delegates appointed by Éamon de Valera, who negotiated and concluded the Treaty signed in London on 6 December 1921, which established the Irish Free State (now the Republic). This was an event of historic significance and the ramifications and consequences of the Treaty are still with us today. The negotiators were Edmund Duggan, Michael Collins, Arthur Griffiths, Robert Barton and George Gavan Duffy. The card was signed by Michael Collins on 18 January 1922.

THE KING AND QUEEN IN IRELAND. JULY, 1903.
ENTRY INTO DUBLIN WITH VICEROY.

King Edward VII and Queen Alexandra, with the Viceroy, in an open carriage entering Dublin in July 1903. The King was popular with Dubliners and cheering crowds line the way.

A garden party with King Edward VII and Queen Alexandra at the Viceregal Lodge in Phoenix Park on 10 July 1907. Earlier that day, the king had visited the Irish International Exhibition at Ballsbridge. However, this 1907 state visit is also remembered for the theft of the Irish Crown Jewels. They were stolen from Dublin Castle just before the visit and they have never been recovered.

An Irish Language Procession at Smithfield, Dublin, on Sunday 12 March 1905. The banner above the speaker's platform proclaims 'The Glory of God and the Honour of Ireland'. The sender of the postcard says how pleased he was to be part of the large crowd, who marched in processional order through the streets of Dublin.

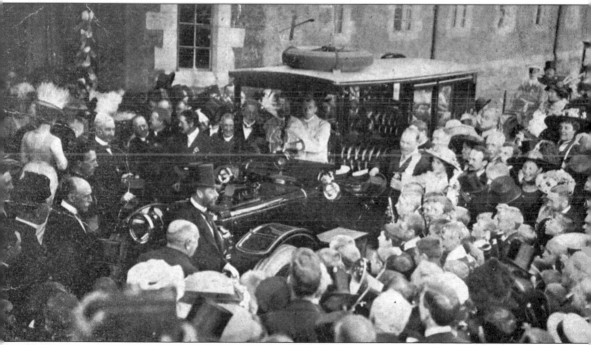

King George V addressing the Band of the Artane Industrial School from Beaumont at Maynooth on Sunday 9 July 1911. This school for boys opened in 1870 and was run by the Christian Brothers. The school became renowned for its band, formed in 1872, which performed to a very high standard. The band's annual programme still includes regular appearances at Croke Park.

The main entrance of the Irish International Exhibition, 1907. This was held on a 52-acre site at Herbert Park, Ballsbridge. It was opened by The Earl of Aberdeen, Lord Lieutenant, on 4 May and closed on 9 November 1907. The exhibition had a large central hall covering 23 acres and had many attractions including a concert hall and palaces of arts and industry. It attracted many visitors and was a great success.

A view in the Palace of Industries, with the assistants and exhibitors at a stand selling glassware and objects of fine art. The exhibitors at the stand are Kyoto and K.A. Jishima, who had previously shown their goods at exhibitions held at St Louis in 1904, Liège in 1905 and Milan in 1906.

Water Chute I.I.E.

The Water Chute, which was a favourite with visitors of all ages at the exhibition. The boat would glide down the long wooden ramp to hit the water with a great spurt of spray. In the background the central building displays Lemco and Oxo advertisements and, on its left, another smaller building promotes Chivers' jams and marmalade.

The Helter-Skelter lighthouse with visitors waiting to take a turn on the slide. The fashions of the time for the ladies must have caused some difficulties coming down the helter-skelter.

Opening of the Royal Dublin Fusiliers' Memorial Arch on 19 August 1907, showing the Duke of Connaught, the Lord Lieutenant and Countess of Aberdeen and Lord Grenfell. The Arch commemorates the Dublin Fusiliers who fought in the Boer War. Republicans called it 'Traitors' Gate'. Lady Aberdeen, a supporter of Home Rule, founded the Women's National Health Association and she arranged for the first supplies of sterilized milk in the city to combat tuberculosis.

The unveiling of the Parnell Monument in Upper O'Connell Street on 1 October 1911, on the twentieth anniversary of his death. Huge crowds gathered to watch the ceremony. At the base of the tall granite obelisk was a statue of Parnell, designed by Augustus St Gaudens. The statue shows Parnell standing with arms outstretched in oratorical pose, surprisingly wearing two overcoats.

A Home Rule demonstration in Dublin on 31 March 1912. John Redmond MP is shown addressing the crowds, said to total 170,000, in O'Connell Street. The sign 'Ireland a Nation' is above the large No. 1 platform. The speakers on other platforms included John Dillon, Joe Devlin and James Swift MacNeill.

Riots took place on Sunday 31 August 1913 in O'Connell Street. James Larkin, the Labour leader, wearing a beard as a disguise, spoke to striking tramway workers from the balcony of the Imperial Hotel on O'Connell Street. An order had been made by the Chief Divisional Magistrate for Dublin, E.G. Swifte, banning any assembly. The police, in some panic, charged the crowd using their batons indiscriminately. Over 600 people were treated in hospital for injuries.

Irish Volunteers in full uniform and with fixed bayonets, parading through the streets of Dublin in February 1916. As a result of poor social conditions in Dublin and following the 1913 'lock-out', James Connolly and the Citizen Army together with Patrick Pearse of Sinn Féin and the Irish Republican Brotherhood had expanded the Volunteer Movement with a view to an armed rising against British rule in Ireland.

Members of the Irish Citizen Army, a labour militia, are shown on the rooftop of Liberty Hall, their headquarters (see also p. 69). Although the Easter Rising in 1916, in which they took part, had no real prospect of military success, it proved to be one of the decisive turning points in Irish history.

Irish Rebellion. May 1916.
Soldiers holding a Dublin Street.

British soldiers holding Talbot Street against the rebels using a very makeshift barricade with furniture taken from houses. The message on the card says that the soldier crouching in the doorway is Charlie Hewitt.

Sinn Fein Rebellion, Dublin
Priests asked to produce their Papers

Priests in overcoats and top hats were stopped by soldiers and asked to produce their papers. They were under suspicion as rebel sympathisers.

British soldiers with bayonets searching a hay-cart for rebels or ammunition.

Irish Rebellion, May, 1916.
Searching a Hay-cart for Rebels or Ammunition.

British soldiers at the Royal Barracks, standing by the normal type of armoured car used in the revolt.

An armoured motor wagon in Bachelors Walk. Specially constructed during the Rebellion, this car used heavy armour plating to protect against snipers. It had been built in eight hours at an engineering yard in Dublin. On the left is G. Butler & Sons, musical instrument makers (see p. 70).

Liberty Hall after the bombardment. The building was held until the Wednesday, when it was bombarded with heavy artillery from Tara Street. The gunboat *Helga* on the Liffey also joined in the bombardment, but had problems as the Loop-Line Bridge was in the way.

The interior of part of the Order Room for G. Butler & Sons, musical instrument makers at Monument House, Bachelor's Walk, after artillery fire. The adjoining premises was Kelly & Son's gun and ammunition shop sited at the corner of Bachelor's Walk and O'Connell Street. Both shops came under heavy fire from a nine-pounder gun firing up D'Olier Street.

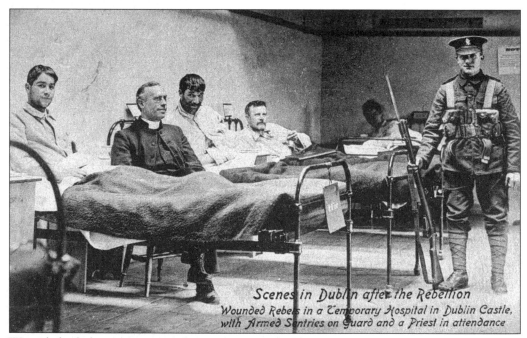

Wounded rebels in a temporary hospital ward in Dublin Castle with an armed sentry on guard and a priest in attendance (see also p. 50).

Friends visiting Sinn Féin prisoners in the Richmond Barracks. Prisoners were allowed visits from their relatives three times a week. Some of the rebels were detained in the Richmond Barracks. However, many were deported to Britain and interned without trial under the Defence of the Realm Acts. About 1,600 men were interned at Frongoch Camp in North Wales. Michael Collins was initially sent to Stafford Prison, but was later transferred to Frongoch Camp.

The Countess Markiewicz seen seated with a female warder in a Red Cross wagon, which took her away after court-martial. She had been sentenced to death, but this was later commuted to life imprisonment. However, she was released from jail under the general amnesty in June 1917. In the General Election of 1918, she became the first woman ever elected to the British House of Commons, but she refused to take her seat.

The review of the Dublin Volunteer Training Corps and St John and Red Cross Ambulance units in College Park, by General Sir John Grenfell Maxwell on Saturday 20 May 1916. He thanked the units for all they had done during the Rising. The photograph shows, from left to right: General Sir John Maxwell, Lady Wimborne, Mr H.H. Asquith (the Prime Minister), Mrs Grosvenor, Mr Bonham Carter, Mr Asquith's private secretary and General Friend.

The Irish Convention in Dublin, 19 April 1917. After the 1916 Rising, Lloyd George made several attempts to get an Irish settlement. One of these was to set up a Convention of about 100 delegates, representing all political parties, under the chairmanship of Sir Horace Plunkett, who had been Liberal Unionist MP for South Dublin from 1892 to 1900. The assembly met regularly until 5 April 1918 and produced a plan for self-government. However, this plan had no chance of success due to the opposition of Sinn Féin, who boycotted the Conference, and the Ulster Unionists.

Funeral of Thomas Ashe at Glasnevin Cemetery on 30 September 1917. Thomas Ashe was leader of North County Dublin Volunteers in the Rising, winning the skirmish of Ashbourne. He was sentenced to death, commuted to penal servitude for life and released under amnesty in June 1917. However, he was rearrested following a speech he made in Co. Longford and sent to Mountjoy Prison. There he went on hunger strike and, despite attempts to force feed him, he died in the Mater Hospital on 25 September 1917.

The Custom House in flames on 25 May 1921, after the Republicans set fire to the Revenue Commissioners' records.

A cloud of smoke hangs over the Liffey after the mine explosion in the Four Courts on 30 June 1922. The bombardment of the Republicans, who refused to evacuate the building, began on Wednesday 28 June. The National Troops used an eighteen-pounder gun mounted on an armoured car sited on the opposite side of the river. All day Thursday the battle continued. However, the following day, the Republicans detonated a landmine under the Central Hall, before surrendering and leaving the building. Irreplaceable records were destroyed, and the effects of the blast were felt in houses up to two miles away.

The front page of the *News of the World* for Sunday 2 July 1922. The headlines describe the battle in the heart of Dublin with Republicans besieged in their headquarters at the Four Courts.

National Army Reserves at a street barricade in July 1922. The barricade does not appear to be very substantial.

National forces bombing Republicans in the Hammam Hotel on Upper O'Connell Street. However, on Tuesday 4 July, an eighteen-pounder gun was placed at the corner of Henry Street from which position the Hammam Hotel and adjoining premises were shelled. By the following day, the buildings were destroyed and the Republicans were forced to surrender.

An armoured Lancia lorry at the corner of Henry Street firing on Republicans in the Gresham and Hammam Hotels.

Upper O'Connell Street, Dublin; after the fighting 1922

Crowds in Upper O'Connell Street after the fighting, looking at the wrecked buildings. There was much destruction and to the right are the remains of the Hammam Hotel, the GPO, the Granville Hotel and the Gresham Hotel. In fact, the wreckage from the 1916 Rebellion in Lower O'Connell Street had still not been all cleared away (also see p. 84).

A benediction on Watling Street Bridge (now Rory O'More Bridge) to celebrate the centenary of Catholic Emancipation, 23 June 1929. Dubliners were in celebratory mood. One hundred years before, on 14 April 1829, the Duke of Wellington, by birth an Anglo-Irish Protestant, had helped carry an Emancipation Bill through Parliament giving Catholics equal rights. Following this act, some Catholics, including Daniel O'Connell, entered Parliament and in the following years many new Catholic churches were built in Ireland.

Catholic Emancipation Centenary, 1929: a procession in Phoenix Park with a military guard of honour for the Blessed Sacrament. The Cardinal Primate of Ireland presided at High Mass in the park, attended by half a million people, to celebrate the Centenary.

Cardinal Lorenzo Lauri, the Papal Legate, arrived in Dublin on 20 June 1932 for the Eucharistic Congress and he was given a grand reception. His carriage was escorted into town by the Free State Hussars, a cavalry corps resplendent in sealskin busbies with plumes, wearing blue uniforms with gold braid and carrying swords. The photograph shows the Cardinal with members of his suite on the balcony at Archbishop House.

The thirty-first International Eucharistic Congress, 22-26 June 1932, was organized by the Catholic Church to promote devotion to the Blessed Sacrament. Pilgrims came from all over the world. Seven ocean liners moored in Dublin Port and provided accommodation for their passengers during the Congress. An altar was sited on O'Connell Bridge and crowds lined the Quays for benediction.

The arrival of the Papal Legate in Phoenix Park to celebrate the Pontifical High Mass on the Sunday. Over a million people attended the Mass and 127 special trains had been laid on to bring them to Dublin from all over Ireland. After the mass, people left the park in procession to attend the concluding benediction of the Congress, which was held on O'Connell Bridge in the evening.

The Papal Legate with Éamon de Valera prior to his departure from Ireland. During his visit Cardinal Lauri was conferred with the title of Honorary Freeman of the Cities of Dublin and Kilkenny.

Declaration of the Republic of Ireland by President Sean T. O'Kelly and the Inter-Party Government at the General Post Office on O'Connell Street, Easter 1949.

Nelson's Pillar, which had survived the bombardment from the gunboat *Helga* in 1916, was blown up in the middle of the night on 8 March 1966, during the fiftieth anniversary year of the Easter Rising. It was done professionally and nobody was injured. Those responsible have never been found. The photograph shows how the pedestal was left and that had to be blown up by the Irish Army. The head from Nelson's statue is now in the Dublin Civic Museum.

Four

Sport, People, Health and Recreation

An advertising card for the Dublin Horse Show in 1929. The show was usually held from the first Tuesday in August until the following Saturday at the Royal Dublin Society's Show Grounds at Ballsbridge. This was the first year in which the USA had an official team in the International Military Jumping Contests.

The packed grandstand at the Horse Show in 1905. The Viceregal party are shown on the balcony. Ladies' Day was a great social occasion for the ladies to wear their latest outfits with stunning hats. The men wore suits with top hats, bowlers or boaters.

The parade of horses and riders in the jumping enclosure in 1911, watched by large crowds from the grandstand. The message on the card written to an address in Suffolk says 'Dublin is full and the streets are crowded. This is a lovely show, the most beautiful I ever saw'.

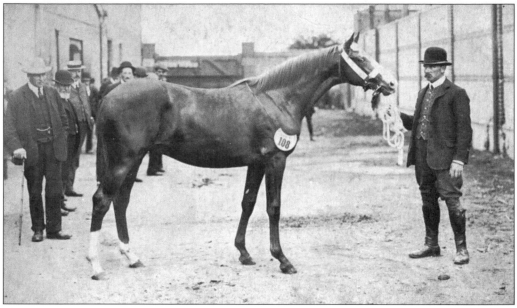

The winner of the first prize and Perpetual Challenge Cup for Thorough-Bred Yearling Colts, owned by Mr M. Smith, on display at the Horse Show in 1905.

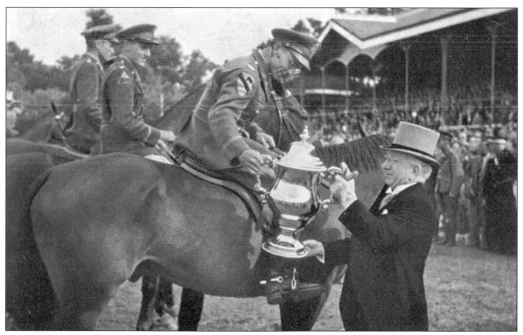

President Sean T. O'Kelly presents the Aga Khan Trophy to the Captain of the USA team in the International Military Jumping Contest at the 1949 Horse Show.

The Thomas Davis Hurling Club, winners of the Junior Championship, Saturday and Sunday Leagues, 1903/04. From left to right, back row: D. O'Callaghan (President), J. Hehir, T. Bolster, J. O'Gorman, M. Larkin, J. Egan, J. Monaghan. Middle row: J. Hensey, D. McInerney, D. Kelleher, M. Jones (Captain), D. Lynch (Vice-Captain), R. Ryan, M. Flanagan, J. Gallagher (Founder). Front row: J. Farrell, S. Considine, J. Kenny, J. Scully.

A Dublin Gaelic football team during the 1920s. The Gaelic sports stadium is Croke Park, where the inter-county All Ireland Football Finals are held in September each year. If Dublin reach the finals, the 'Dubs' supporters stand on 'Hill 16', which is a terrace mainly formed of debris from the ruins of O'Connell Street left in the 1916 Rising and the Civil War.

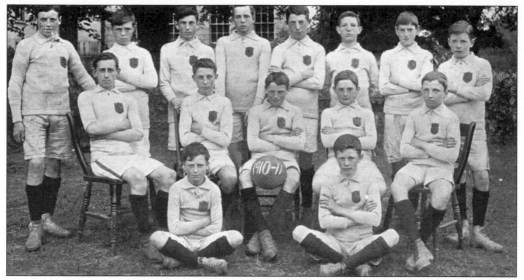

The junior Gaelic football team of St Enda's College, Rathfarnham, holders of the Dublin Schools Cup, 1910/11. St Enda's, an Irish-speaking school, was founded by Patrick Pearse. From left to right, back row: P. Walsh, R. MacAuliffe, B. O'Toole, S. MacDermot, S. Dowling, P. Molloy, C. MacKinley, F. Doherty. Middle row: S. Doyle, B. Joyce, F. Burke, U. Houlihan, B. Cleary. Front row: C. Cleary, S. O'Connor.

St Enda's College junior hurling team, holders of the Dublin Schools Cup in 1910/11. From left to right, back row: S. O'Connor, P. Walsh, R. MacAuliffe, B. O'Toole, S. Doyle, S. Dowling, E. McDavid, C. MacKinley. Middle row: U. Houlihan, S. MacDermott, B. Joyce, U. O'Toole, T. Horan. Front row: S. Horan, S. Power.

Shelbourne Football Club, runners-up for the Irish Cup in the 1904/05 season. From left to right, back row: Pidgeon, Penston, Doherty, Ronan (treasurer), Abbey, Kelly, Monks (trainer), Cunningham (secretary). Middle row: Wimble, Jack Owens, Heslin, James Owens, Ledwidge. Front row: Lawless, Cleary.

Shelbourne Football Club, winners of the Irish Cup in 1911. From left to right, back row: -?-, W. Watson, H. Owens, W. Rowe, J. O'Brien, P. Quinn (trainer). Middle row : R. Merrigan (linesman), J. Stothers, J. Clarkin, J. Moran (captain), L. Devlin, J. Dunn, J. Westby. Front row (sitting): J. Bennett, J. Murphy.

The Ireland football team, which beat England 3-0 in 1914. Back row : H. Hegan (IFA), A. Jackson (referee), H. Hampton, P. O'Connell (Captain), F. McKee, M. Hamill, W. McConnell, A. Craif, J. Clarke (IFA), R. Kirkpatrick (IFA). Middle row: D.W. Foy, D. Rollo, S. Young, W. Gillespie, W. Lacey, F. Thompson, R. Torrans. Front row: R. Norwood. International matches between England and Ireland were played annually from 1882. The Irish matches were played in Belfast, apart from 1900 and 1912, which took place in Dublin. Ireland's first victory was in 1913.

The Dublin University (Past and Present) cricket team which played the Australian touring team at College Park in June 1905. From left to right, back row: P.A. Meldon, R.M. Gwynn, H.H. Corley, E. Ensor, A.L. Leeper, J.T. Gwynnn. Front row: S.D. Lambert, C.R. Faussett, F.H. Browning, Revd T.A. Harvey, J.E. Lynch.

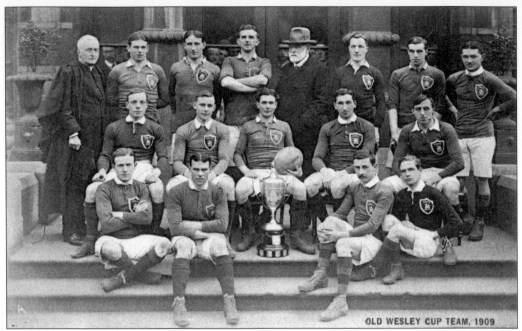

Old Wesley rugby football team, winners of the Leinster Senior Cup in 1909.

The Irish rugby team which triumphed over England by 6 points to 3 at Lansdowne Road on 8 February 1936. From left to right, back row: L.A. Bailey (Lansdowne), S. Deering (Bective Rangers), H.J. Sayers (Army), R. Alexander (Northern Ireland), L.B. McMahon (University College, Dublin), L.M. Malcolmson (Northern Ireland), S.T. Irwin (President, IRU). Front row: C.R. Graves (Wanderers), F.G. Moran (Clontarf), J. Russell (University College, Cork), J.A. Siggins (Captain) (Collegians), C.E. Beamish (Harlequins), S. Walker (Instonians), V. Hewitt (Instonians). Seated: C.V. Boyle (Dublin University), G.J. Morgan (Clontarf).

Castleknock College rugby team – winners of the Leinster Senior Schools Cup in 1913.

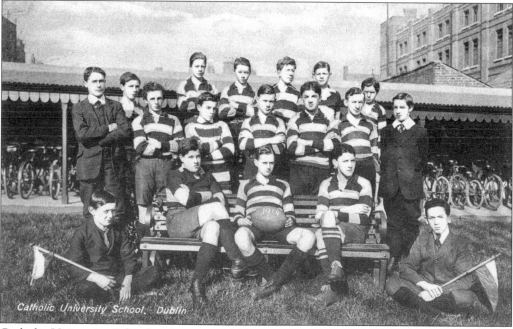

Catholic University School rugby team, 1914.

Castleknock College Tennis Tournament prize winners, 1913.

Winners of the All Ireland Junior Challenge Shield for gymnastics (presented by Leahy, Kelly & Leahy Ltd) in 1908.

Jem Roche (5ft 8ins and weighing 13st 7lbs) was the Irish heavyweight boxing champion. He was a Wexford blacksmith, who in his teens played Gaelic football for Wexford United. He fought for the World title against the Canadian Tommy Burns at the Theatre Royal in Hawkins Street, Dublin, on 17 March 1908. The match was a sell-out and 3,000 people packed the theatre. Unfortunately, Jem was knocked out in round one after 86 seconds.

Jim Coffey, the Dublin Giant Boxer. He was born in 1891 in Roscommon, but moved to Dublin and emigrated to America as a young man. He was 6ft 3 ins tall and weighed 15st and had a good punch, scoring twenty-three knockout wins in his six-year career. In sixty-two fights, he was beaten only four times. He was the Irish 'Great White Hope', tipped to win the title from the first black world heavyweight champion, Jack Johnson. Unfortunately, an American, Jack Moran, ended the dream by defeating him in October 1915 and in the return match in January 1916. Coffey returned to Ireland in 1921 and died in Dublin on 20 December 1959.

A First Communion class at the Sisters of Mercy School, Booterstown, Dublin, in 1949. From left to right, back row: Henry Haughton, -?-, Paddy Grace, -?-, Michael Slattery, Tommy Murphy. Middle row: Pat Ennnis, -?-, Pat Clark, Canon Flanagan, -?-, Owen Byrne, David Harlow, Michael Dunne. Front row: M. Mullen, Peter O'Hara, Mick Lean, -?-, Charlie Byrne.

Class 2 Primary at the Christian Brothers' School, Westland Row, 1950.

Confirmation class at Scoil Mhuire Christian Brothers' School, Griffith Avenue, Marino, 1955.

Confirmation class at the St Vincent de Paul School for Girls, Griffith Avenue, Marino, 1958.

A group of Scouts from St Jude's, Dublin, on pilgrimage to Lourdes in August 1962.

Confirmation class at Scoil Mhuire Christian Brothers' School, Griffith Avenue, Marino, 1963.

A class from St Assam's School, Raheny, making their First Holy Communion in 1955.

The parish committee of St Assam's church, Raheny, c. 1960. From left to right, back row: Tommy Duffy, Tommy Gibson, Paddy MacAlister, Stephen Grace, John Fenlon, Peter Cooling, Dinny Dwyer. Front row: Mick O'Doherty, Monsignor Fitzpatrick, Paddy Thomas.

Leaving Certificate group at St Joseph's Secondary School, Fairview, in 1966. From left to right, back row: V. Flood, S. Daly, T. Peteridge, F. MacAlister, B. Rice, D. Dowling. Third row: M. Lynch, -?-, B. Healey, N. Cahill, T. Dunne, M. Egan, -?-, -?-. Second row: P. Cashin, -?-, M. Prior, S. Daly, -?-, K. Slattery, J. Hickey, C. Barrett. Front row: S. O'Fee, P. Molloy, T. Cahill, C. O'Sullivan, C. Hyland, P. Tierney, B. Daly, K. Martin, -?-.

Production of *The Quaker Girl* by girls from the fourth year at Our Lady of Mercy College, Beaumont, in November 1963.

P.T. Durney, Champion Ball Walker of the World. He had walked on the large ball from Dublin to Belfast, said to be a distance of 150 miles, in April 1910. He could not have taken a direct route. The card states that he received £500 for this extraordinary deed.

Crowds gather in O'Connell Street in 1940 to welcome Gene Autrey, the singing cowboy, who was appearing at the Theatre Royal. His visit created great excitement and the shows were a sell-out.

A coalman on his cart delivering coal from S.N. Robinson & Co., 21 City Quay. In 1906, another coalman, Patrick O'Carroll, had been fined for displaying his name illegibly on his cart. However, the name was written in Irish, so he refused to pay any fine. In the end, the Court seized a ton of coal from him to pay the fine.

A very smart Lady Lena and cart from Boland's Bakery, Dublin. They were winners of the First Prize (class 107), Silver Cup and also the Challenge Silver Cup at the Royal Dublin Show at Ballsbridge in 1911.

Embroidery at Dun Emer Industries, Dublin Depot, 28 Clare Street, September 1905. The Yeats sisters worked as a partnership making fine vestments and embroidered banners. One set designed by the painter Jack Yeats was made for Loughrea Cathedral, with scenes of Irish saints. The sender of the card, Elizabeth Yeats, invites her friend to come with her to see brother Jack's pictures, if she is in Dublin on the Saturday afternoon.

Grinding department at Booth Brothers' Engineers' Supplies, 13 Pembroke Row, Dublin.

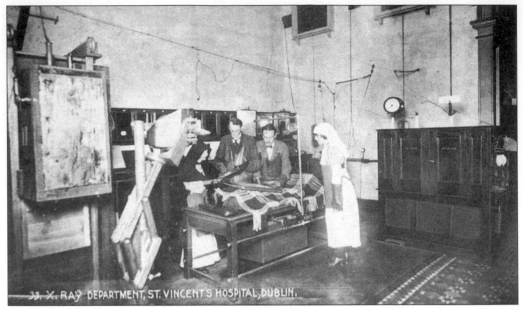

X RAY DEPARTMENT, ST. VINCENT'S HOSPITAL, DUBLIN.

St Vincent's Hospital was opened on St Stephen's Green by the Irish Sisters of Charity in 1834, and was to remain there until November 1970. This view, postmarked August 1922, shows the X-ray Department at the Hospital. An X-ray plate is held over the patient by the formally dressed Dr Michael O'Hea, radiologist, and his assistant. Small aprons are the only protective clothing worn. Before his appointment to St Vincent's, Dr O'Hea had been Assistant Physician to the Children's Hospital, Temple Street.

The Children's Hospital, Temple Street, run by the Irish Sisters of Charity, was opened in 1879, moving from premises known as St Joseph's Infirmary in Buckingham Street. The photograph shows the sun balconies at the hospital. At that time, in the pre-antibiotic era, the favourite treatment to cure children's illnesses, including tuberculosis, was 'Fresh air, sunshine and Bird's Custard'.

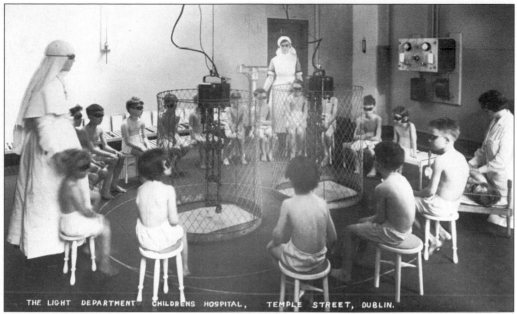

The Light Department, Children's Hospital, Temple Street. 'Artificial sunshine' was used to treat various childhood conditions. Doctors were not aware of all the possible side-effects including skin cancer in later life, although the staff and children did wear goggles to protect their eyes.

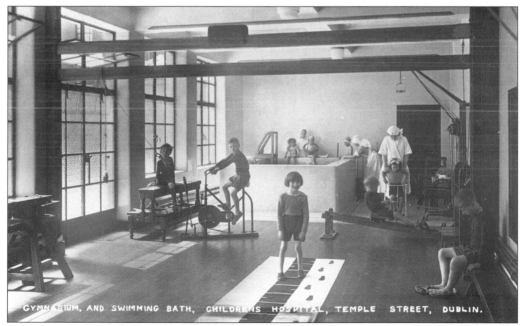

Gymnasium and swimming bath at the Children's Hospital, Temple Street. These facilities were particularly valuable as exercise and hydrotherapy were of great help to children with cerebral palsy and mobility problems.

Strawberry Beds, Dublin

In the summertime, the strawberry beds near Castleknock were a popular destination for Dubliners, who would have a pleasant day out picking strawberries. The southern facing slopes and rich soil produced excellent fruit. There was also good fishing in the River Liffey.

The Floating Ballroom on the Liffey, moored below Butt Bridge, *c.* 1930. The Loopline Railway Bridge can be seen in the background. Dubliners loved dancing, and although it was not on the same scale as the Gresham, Metropole or Shelbourne Hotels, the Floating Ballroom was still a popular venue. In times past, there had been a floating chapel for seamen on the Liffey, moored at Ringsend from 1823 to 1832.

The Zoological Gardens in Phoenix Park opened in 1831, making it one of the oldest zoos in the world. It is well known for breeding lions, including the lion which roars at the start of Metro Goldwyn Mayer films. A visit to the zoo must be one of the favourite leisure activities of all Dubliners. Here, in the 1950s, it is very crowded and children enjoy a ride on Sarah, the Indian elephant.

A POLO MATCH AT PHOENIX PARK, DUBLIN.

A polo match at Phoenix Park in July 1928. This is one of the few places in the world where polo can be watched without charge.

Crowds watch rally car racing at the Phoenix Park in the 1960s.

Enthusiasts gather around a Mini competing in the car rally. Standing from left to right: Noel Smith (driver), -?-, -?-, Jimmy Nolan, Mike Corbett.

Five
Around the Suburbs

Lourdes Grotto, Inchicore. The unveiling ceremony was held on 12 May 1930. The grotto was at the rear of the Church of Mary Immaculate, attached to the Oblate retreat house. Loyalty to the church and religious observance at the time was very strong.

The entrance gates to the Phoenix Park from the North Circular Road, *c.* 1920. The Toll House tea rooms and the Phoenix Park Café are seen on the right. Children run on the road without fear of traffic. The road was three miles long and extended to the North Wall. It was one of the boundary roads encircling Dublin and together with the South Circular Road, it was laid down in 1763.

The Cattle Market on the North Circular Road, *c.* 1930. Cattle can be seen in the pens in the foreground and sheep in the distant pens. The market was held weekly and afterwards the cattle, sheep and pigs were driven down the North Circular Road to the North Wall. The exodus regularly held up the traffic. In *Ulysses*, Bloom's funeral cab was delayed on its way to Glasnevin Cemetery by beasts from the market.

A busy scene in Phibsborough, *c.* 1910. The early Gothic-style St Peter's church, designed by George Goldie in 1869, is seen on the left. The spire dates from 1907. The drays are outside the Bohemian Bar delivering barrels of Guinness. The entrance to the Bohemian Football Club at Dalymount Park is near to the church at No. 72 North Circular Road. A policeman stands on the corner, perhaps waiting to hold up traffic so that funerals could progress easily to the cemetery.

Prospect Road, which runs from Phibsborough past Glasnevin Cemetery, *c.* 1905. The writer of the postcard complains at the state of the road and path, which she uses night and morning to go to and from Talbot House. The road is very basic, suitable only for carts, and has not been tarred. However, the card does show a workman sweeping the road!

Chapel from Entrance
Glasnevin Dublin

The gatekeeper and visitors gather at the entrance to Glasnevin or Prospect Cemetery. The land had been bought by the Burial Committee of the Catholic Association in September 1831. However, the cemetery was constantly under threat from body-snatchers. The cemetery had watchtowers and was patrolled by Cuban bloodhounds. Unfortunately, in 1853 the bloodhounds attacked Dr Kirwan, the Dublin City Coroner, and after this, the dogs were no longer used for security.

Chapel and O'Connell Monument
Glasnevin, Dublin

A father and his children pose by the little mortuary chapel of white granite designed by J. McCarthy and built in 1878. This was similar to Cormac's chapel on the Rock of Cashel in Tipperary. Adjacent is the Round Tower, built in 1869, which rises above the vault containing the coffin of the 'Liberator', Daniel O'Connell.

A pauper's funeral at Glasnevin, c. 1910. The plain hearse drawn by a solitary horse waits outside the chapel. This contrasts with the usual funerals, which had fine hearses with many grieving friends and relatives in long procession. By 1900, at Glasnevin there were about 14,000 paid-up burials taking place each year, with about 2,500 paupers interred in 'Poor Ground'.

A bill from C.W. Harrison & Sons, Architectural and Monumental Sculptors, at 178 Great Brunswick Street, dated 5 March 1908, to supply a high granite Celtic Cross for the sum of £9 – a considerable amount at that time. Coffin makers were concentrated in this area and also Cook Street, near Christchurch. All coffin sheds were left open to the public, as people would not steal coffins, as they could not be pawned.

View in Garrai Na Lus—Botanic Gardens. Dublin.

The Botanic Gardens, Glasnevin. These were founded by the Royal Dublin Society in 1795 on land purchased from the family of the poet, Thomas Tickell. The design was based on Kew Gardens. In the early nineteenth century, the gardens were among the largest and most beautiful in Europe. The many Victorian glasshouses were built during the 1850s. Dubliners have always flocked to the gardens in great numbers. It is recorded that on one Sunday in August 1861 over 15,000 visitors came to the gardens.

Tolka Bridge, Glasnevin, *c*. 1913. The writer of the postcard says it was the spot where she caught her biggest fish on holiday. This was a prosperous area and in the nineteenth century it was a favourite summer residence for visitors to Dublin. The first building over the bridge is the Glasnevin post office.

Drumcondra, Dublin

Lower Drumcondra Road, *c*. 1927. In the past Drumcondra was a haunt of highwaymen and smugglers. The No. 17 tram has stopped near the bridge over the River Tolka. A short distance away, heading into town on the left side of the road, is Holy Cross College and the residential Palace of the Catholic Archbishop of Dublin.

During the Second World War there was a part-time reserve force to prevent any invasion of neutral Ireland, in which a total of 250,000 enrolled. The card shows Alec Ankers, aged seventeen, from Millmount Avenue, Drumcondra in 1942. He wears the uniform of the Local Defence Force, but carries no arms.

111

Principal Linen Machine Room, St Mary's Asylum, High Park Convent, Drumcondra, *c.* 1910. The bed sheets were ironed and folded in this room, which was well staffed.

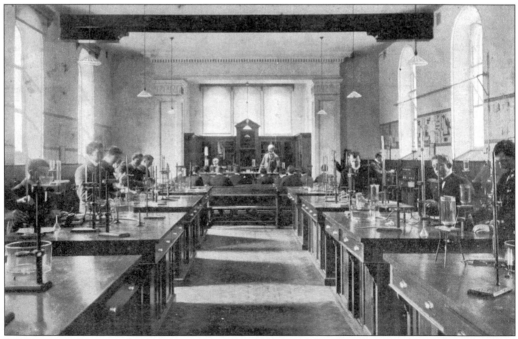

Students working in the science laboratory at St Patrick's Training College, Drumcondra, *c.* 1913. The writer of the card says Professor Foy is giving the lecture at the front of the classroom.

Fair View, Dublin

A quiet scene in Fairview, *c.* 1940. The bakers Johnston, Mooney and O'Brien are on the corner next to Bailey's grocers. The Howth omnibus is seen on the right of the photograph.

The Royal Victoria Eye and Ear Hospital, Adelaide Road, *c.* 1915. This hospital opened in 1904 following the amalgamation of the National Eye and Ear Infirmary and St Mark's Ophthalmic Hospital. In the first year, 1,284 in-patients and 7,230 out-patients were treated. It has continued to thrive as a large specialist centre and has an international reputation.

Harcourt Road *c.* 1910, connects Harrington Street to Adelaide Road. The trams in the centre have just passed under the railway bridge. Barnes newsagents, which is the Harcourt Road post office, is on the left with a weighing machine outside.

Harcourt Road at the junction with Harcourt Street, *c.* 1935. On the right, barefoot young boys outside the chemist's are peeping round the corner. Edward Carson, the Ulster Unionist leader, was born at No. 4 Harcourt Street. Cardinal Newman used to live at No. 6, which later became the headquarters of the Sinn Féin movement.

The Grand Canal from Clanbrassil Street Bridge, showing Griffiths Barracks, c. 1940. A barge is coming up the canal and turf is piled high on the quay. The canal connected the ports of Dublin, Limerick and Waterford, terminating in the Grand Canal Dock, which adjoined the South Quays and meets with the Liffey, where it is joined by the River Dodder.

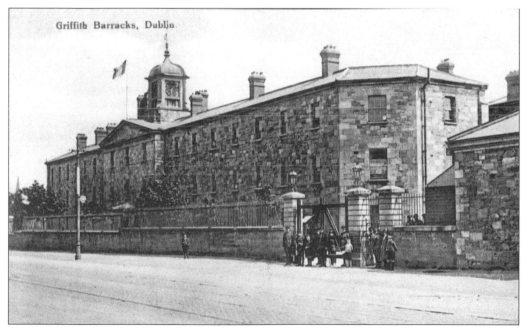

Griffiths (Wellington) Barracks was initially built to be a remand prison, but was transferred to the War Department in 1877, and in 1892, the Royal Munster Fusiliers were stationed there. In 1922, it was the second barracks, after Beggars' Bush, to be occupied by Irish troops.

Portobello Harbour, Rathmines, *c.* 1910. The harbour was built by the Grand Canal Company to allow barges and boats to moor at Portobello House, seen on the left. The bridge was the site of the Rathmines horse-drawn omnibus tragedy on 6 April 1861, when a bus and horses on the way to the city from Terenure plunged into the lock. Five passengers including a baby were drowned. The victims included Mrs O'Connell and her daughter, Matilda, who were related to Daniel O'Connell.

THE CANAL, RATHMINES, DUBLIN

Another view of boats on the Canal in 1922. Portobello House, on the opposite bank, was originally built as a hotel by the Grand Canal Company. It opened in July 1807 and continued as a hotel until 1860, when it was sold to the Sisters of Charity and used as a home for the blind until 1868. From 1898 to 1971, it was a private nursing home. The painter, Jack B. Yeats (1871-1957, see p. 99) spent his last years there.

Rathmines, c. 1904. This was a prosperous residential area and until the Greater Dublin Act of 1930, it was a separate municipality with a population of 70,000. The tram bound for the city centre is about to pass the splendid Town Hall built in 1887. It was from the Italianate clock tower in 1896 that Marconi demonstrated the wireless telegraph. A collection van for the London and North Western Railway is on the right, outside Meyers & Sons.

Rathmines, c. 1947. The No. 15 Terenure tram, advertising Boland's Bakeries and Tyler's for Shoes is picking up passengers. Rathmines remains a pleasant busy suburban shopping area, although the shops have changed and now Raleigh 'all-steel' bicycles are for sale.

The shop front for Kearns, jeweller and watchmaker on Rathmines Road. There is an impressive window display. Spectacles and eye glasses are also for sale, and the shop acts as agent for Royal Ediswan Lamps.

Lower Rathmines Road, c. 1916. The photographer has attracted interest from the group of young boys on the right and also the lady in the shop doorway on the left. The boys may be waiting to go to the Rathmines cinema, whose sign projects over the pavement on the right.

The Orwell Bridge, on the River Dodder, Rathmines, *c.* 1920. The barefoot boy on the pathway poses for the photographer.

Dartry Dye Works on the River Dodder, Upper Rathmines, *c.* 1910. The site was previously occupied by Williams' cloth mill, built in 1844. There was a water wheel on the Dodder, which was only removed in 1950.

Ranelagh Road, from the Grand Canal Bridge, *c.* 1927. One young boy has climbed the lamp post for a better look at the photographer. On summer days, groups of boys would often go swimming in the canal.

Ranelagh, *c.* 1917. Gordon's, the chandler and ironmonger, is the shop on the corner. Next door is the Dublin Laundry Co. Ltd and the Dartry Dye Works Ltd (see p. 119). The greengrocer, J. & H. Menery, displays produce on the pavement.

A quiet scene on Ranelagh Road, *c.* 1910. The trams are strangely absent. Perhaps the aim of the card publisher was to focus attention on the sign for the Singer shop at No. 4.

A peaceful scene in Donnybrook Village, *c.* 1910. This was not always the case as the Donnybrook Fair, held here each year from 1204, until it was suppressed in 1855, had a reputation for bacchanalian debauchery and drunkenness.

The bridge over the Dodder at Ballsbridge, *c.* 1916. The message on the back of this card refers to an ambush of the Sherwood Foresters on 26 April 1916 on their way from Kingstown. This occurred further down this road, at Mount Street Bridge over the Grand Canal, and there were many casualties.

Upper Baggot Street, *c.* 1905. The view shows the bridge over the Grand Canal built in 1790 and named after John McCartney, the chairman of the Grand Canal Company. The Hibernian Bank is on the corner. A little further down the road on the left is the Royal City of Dublin Hospital.

The Royal City of Dublin Hospital, c. 1905. The hospital opened in 1832 with fifty-two beds. On the foundation of the Nurses' Home by Princess Christian of Schleswig-Holstein in 1900, 'Royal' was added to the hospital's title. It was not until 1904 that the hospital had electric light fitted, at a cost of £434. In the 1916 rebellion over 200 Irish casualties were treated at Baggot Street. The hospital closed in June 1986, but was re-opened as a community hospital in January 1988.

The Open-Air School at Ballsbridge, May 1911. The purpose of this type of school was to encourage children to learn Gaelic.

Merrion Road, Ballsbridge, *c.* 1920. The Town Hall for the then independent Pembroke township is on the right and next to it is the entrance to the Royal Dublin Society's show grounds. The Royal Dublin Society was founded in 1731 for the advancement of agriculture, industry, science and art, and it continues to play an important part in the commercial and cultural life of Ireland.

The Central Hall at the Royal Dublin Society's Annual Spring Show and Irish Industries Fair at Ballsbridge, *c.* 1920. The stands display the wares of many well-known Dublin traders. This show was very popular with the middle classes, who appreciated the fine selection of 'free samples' given by the exhibitors.

124

Rathgar, *c.* 1910. Christ Church is at the junction of Rathgar Road and Highfield Road. This fine church was designed by the Scottish architect, Andrew Heiton, and was opened in 1859.

Rathgar Road, *c.* 1915. The Church of The Three Patrons is on the left. This was built in 1891. It was intended that the classical façade should have a portico with pillars, but this was never built. The 'three patrons' are Saints Patrick, Brigid and Columcille. Around 1880, James Joyce's parents, John Joyce and Mary Jane Murray, sang in the choir, which was then one of Dublin's finest church choirs.

Cross Roads, Terenure, *c.* 1923. Brady and Sons, wine merchants, are on the corner. This area is said to have bracing air due to its height above sea level. This road was previously said to be level with the summit of Nelson's Pillar.

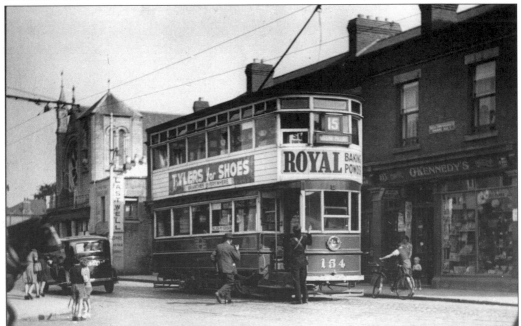

Terenure Road, *c.* 1947. St Joseph's church is on the left of the photograph. This was built in 1904. However, the intended bell tower was not built and the bell now hangs in an iron cage in the church grounds. The church has a very fine stained-glass window, 'The Crucifixion' by the Dublin artist Harry Clarke, whose studio was in North Frederick Street. The No. 15 tram has stopped outside O'Kennedy's to pick up passengers.

Main Street, Rathfarnham, *c.* 1910. The enterprising salesman advertises his services on the back of his van. The village at the 'Gateway to the Dublin Mountains' was well known for its educational establishments including the Jesuit house of studies at Rathfarnham Castle, St Columba's College, St Enda's College (see p. 85) and the Loreto Abbey.

Main Street, Dundrum, *c.* 1910. Brennan's stationers and newsagent is on the right. This village, on the Enniskerry road, was a popular health resort in the nineteenth century.

Tallaght, *c.* 1920. The steam tram from Terenure is seen heading through the village for Blessington. This steam tram, which ran on a track on the side of the road, developed quite a reputation, as so many people carelessly walking on the track were killed and injured each year. In fact, crosses were put up along the track where people had died and the route became known as 'the longest graveyard in Ireland'.

Production of *The Hostage* by Brendan Behan at The Embankment, Tallaght in 1971. Cast, from left to right: Bernadette Short, Colm Meaney, -?-, Christy Hyland, -?-, Eric Erskine, Mary Casey, Gerry ?, Marie Rafferty, Don Foley, Fergal MacAlister, Patricia ?, -?-, Larry ?, -?-, plus three cast members in front.

128